I Can Be Anything!

I CAN BE A SOCCER PLAYER

By Miller Slenzak

Please visit our website, www.garethstevens.com. For a free color catalog of all our high-quality books, call toll free 1-800-542-2595 or fax 1-877-542-2596.

Library of Congress Cataloging-in-Publication Data

Names: Slenzak, Miller, author.
Title: I can be a soccer player / Miller Slenzak.
Description: New York : Gareth Stevens Publishing, 2019. | Series: I can be anything! | Includes index.
Identifiers: LCCN 2017050102| ISBN 9781538217689 (library bound) | ISBN 9781538217702 (pbk.) | ISBN 9781538217719 (6 pack)
Subjects: LCSH: Soccer–Juvenile literature.
Classification: LCC GV943.25 .S48 2019 | DDC 796.334–dc23 LC record available at https://lccn.loc.gov/2017050102

First Edition

Published in 2019 by
Gareth Stevens Publishing
111 East 14th Street, Suite 349
New York, NY 10003

Copyright © 2019 Gareth Stevens Publishing

Editor: Kate Mikoley
Designer: Laura Bowen

Photo credits: Cover, p. 1 (kid) erics/Shutterstock.com; cover, p.1 (background) Fotosr52/Shutterstock.com; p. 5 FatCamera/E+/Getty Images; pp. 7, 24 Hybrid Images/Cultura/Getty Images; p. 9 John Giustina/The Images Bank/Getty Images; p. 11 matimix/Shutterstock.com; p. 13 Catherine Steenkeste/Getty Images Sport; pp. 15, 24 ilbusca/E+/Getty Images; pp. 17, 24 tratong/Shutterstock.com; p. 19 Rob Marmion/Shutterstock.com; p. 21 Icon Sportswire/Getty Images; p. 23 wavebreakmedia/Shutterstock.com.

All rights reserved. No part of this book may be reproduced in any form without permission in writing from the publisher, except by a reviewer.

Printed in the United States of America

CPSIA compliance information: Batch #CS18GS: For further information contact Gareth Stevens, New York, New York at 1-800-542-2595.

Contents

I love soccer!
I play on a team.

This is Mr. Tom.
He's the coach.

A coach is like a teacher.

We learn to kick the ball.

We play for fun.
Some people play
as a job.

12

A goalie blocks the net.
Forwards take
many shots.

A goal is a shot that goes in the net.

We run a lot in soccer.

Many soccer players
can run fast!

26

I can be a soccer player.
So can you!